A NOTE TO PARENTS

When your children are ready to "step into reading," giving them the right books—and lots of them—is as crucial as giving them the right food to eat. **Step into Reading Books** present exciting stories and information reinforced with lively, colorful illustrations that make learning to read fun, satisfying, and worthwhile. They are priced so that acquiring an entire library of them is affordable. And they are beginning readers with an important difference—they're written on four levels.

Step 1 Books, with their very large type and extremely simple vocabulary, have been created for the very youngest readers. **Step 2 Books** are both longer and slightly more difficult. **Step 3 Books,** written to mid-second-grade reading levels, are for the child who has acquired even greater reading skills. **Step 4 Books** offer exciting nonfiction for the increasingly proficient reader.

Children develop at different ages. **Step into Reading Books,** with their four levels of reading, are designed to help children become good—and interested—readers *faster*. The grade levels assigned to the four steps—preschool through grade 1 for Step 1, grades 1 through 3 for Step 2, grades 2 and 3 for Step 3, and grades 2 through 4 for Step 4—are intended only as guides. Some children move through all four steps very rapidly; others climb the steps over a period of several years. These books will help your child "step into reading" in style!

Library of Congress Cataloging-in-Publication Data:
Ehrlich, Amy, 1942— .
Buck-Buck the chicken. (Step into reading. A Step 2 book) SUMMARY: Nancy's pet chicken, Buck-Buck, has trouble learning to act like an ordinary chicken. [1. Chickens—Fiction. 2. Pets—Fiction. 3. Humorous stories] I. Title. II. Series: Step into reading. Step 2 book.   PZ7.E328Bt
1987 [E]   86-31639   ISBN: 0-394-88804-9 (trade); 0-394-98804-3 (lib. bdg.)

Manufactured in the United States of America   8 9 0

STEP INTO READING is a trademark of Random House, Inc.

Step into Reading

BUCK-BUCK
the Chicken

By Amy Ehrlich
Illustrated by R. W. Alley

A Step 2 Book

Random House New York

Buck-Buck is not like

other chickens.

She does not eat corn.

She does not live

in a henhouse.

And she never lays any eggs.

Buck-Buck is

Nancy Smith's pet.

Nancy's father won her

at the county fair.

He guessed the number

of jelly beans

in a jar

and took Buck-Buck home.

Now Buck-Buck lives
on the Smiths' front porch.
"Buck-buck!" she says
each time they come outside.
That is how she got her name.

Buck-Buck likes to go

for walks with the Smiths.

She nods at everyone they pass.

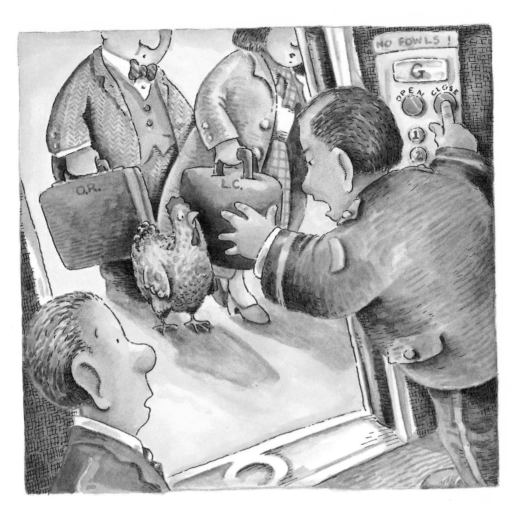

Once she followed Mr. Smith

to his office.

But the elevator man

would not let her in.

"No chickens allowed,"

he said.

Another time Buck-Buck
followed Mrs. Smith
to the dress store.
A woman there
thought she was a hat
and wanted to try her on.
That night the Smiths
had a talk with Nancy
about Buck-Buck.
"Why can't that chicken
stay home and act
more like a chicken?"
asked Mr. Smith.
"Wouldn't you like
a dog or a cat instead?"
asked Mrs. Smith.

But Nancy did not want
a cat or a dog.
"Buck-Buck is my best friend,"
she told her parents.

Buck-Buck lets Nancy
swing her on the swings,

put doll clothes on her,

and take her for rides

in the baby carriage.

"Coochie coochie coo,"
says Nancy.
She tickles Buck-Buck
under her chin.
Buck-Buck blinks with joy.

One day in July
Nancy and Buck-Buck
went to the park.
"Hi," said Liz Martin.
"Can I see your baby?"

"Buck-buck!" said Buck-Buck,
flying out of the carriage.
"What a smart baby!"
Liz said. "Mine hasn't even
started talking yet."

Over the summer

Nancy Smith's friends

got to know Buck-Buck.

She went on picnics with them.

She went swimming at the town pool.

One Saturday in August

Nancy and Billy Gray

took Buck-Buck to the movies.

During the scary parts

Buck-Buck hid under the seat.

"Buck-Buck is chicken,"

Billy said to Nancy.

"Don't you dare call

my chicken chicken!"

cried Nancy.

When fall came

Nancy had to go back to school.

"Be a good chicken

while I'm gone," she said,

waving good-bye to Buck-Buck.

Buck-Buck nodded.

But later when Mrs. Smith

went jogging,

Buck-Buck followed her

for miles.

When Buck-Buck got tired,
she flew onto
Mrs. Smith's head.
Mrs. Smith could not jog
with a chicken on her head.
So she and Buck-Buck
went home.

"That chicken is bored,"
said Mrs. Smith at dinner.
"Maybe she needs
to peck in the dirt
like other chickens."
"Great idea!" said Mr. Smith.
And he took Buck-Buck
with him into the garden.
All evening long
he hoed and raked
while Buck-Buck ate the weeds.

But the next day
when nobody was home,
Buck-Buck went gardening
by herself.

That was the end
of the vegetables.

"Maybe she's just young,"
said Mrs. Smith.

"Let's give her another chance."

"Goody!" said Nancy Smith.

"That means she can come
to my birthday party."

"She'd better behave,"
said Mrs. Smith.

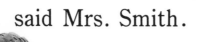
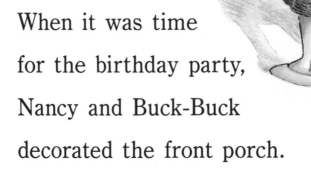

When it was time
for the birthday party,
Nancy and Buck-Buck
decorated the front porch.

Buck-Buck loved the balloons.

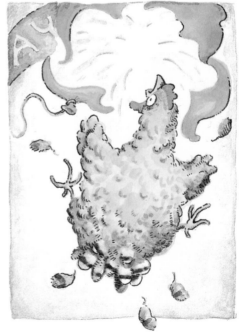

She popped every one.

"What's all that noise?"
asked Mr. Smith.
"I didn't hear anything,"
said Nancy.
She and Buck-Buck
put on their party hats
and waited for the kids to come.

The first was Joey James.

He knew Buck-Buck.

But his mother

had never seen her.

Buck-Buck ran to meet them.

"Buck-buck! Buck-buck!"

she said,

flying up and down.

"Attack chicken!
Attack chicken!"
yelled Mrs. James.
She hid behind a tree.

Mr. and Mrs. Smith ran outside.
As soon as Buck-Buck saw them,
she hid behind the tree too.
"Please forgive our chicken,"
said Mrs. Smith to Mrs. James.
"This is her first
birthday party."

When all the kids arrived,
there was ice cream and cake.
Then they played musical chairs.
Buck-Buck wanted to play too.

She flew from chair to chair
and would not let
anyone sit down.

During hide-and-seek

Buck-Buck gave away

all the hiding places.

Then everyone played
pin the tail on the donkey.
Buck-Buck pulled
the tail off the donkey!

"I forgot to tell her

the rules," said Nancy.

"I'm sorry," Mr. Smith said.

"That chicken has been bad

once too often."

And he locked Buck-Buck

out of the house.

There was nothing more
Nancy could say.
She opened her presents.
Then everyone watched cartoons
on the Smiths' VCR.

"Buck-buck, buck-buck!"
called Buck-Buck
from the porch.
She made so much noise
that Mr. Smith
closed the windows.
Now it was quiet.

But when the birthday party
was over,
Buck-Buck was gone.

"I want my Buck-Buck!"
cried Nancy.
"We hurt her feelings,"
said Mrs. Smith.

The Smiths looked all around.
No one had seen Buck-Buck
at the supermarket,

the firehouse,

the laundry,

or the police station.

But everyone wanted to help.

Soon people were walking

all over town

looking for Nancy's chicken.

38

But when it got dark,
Buck-Buck was still missing.
The Smiths were very sad.
They sat together
on the porch steps
talking about Buck-Buck.
"Maybe I was too hard on her,"
said Mr. Smith.
"She didn't know any better,"
said Mrs. Smith.
"Buck-Buck was my best friend,"
said Nancy.
"She always knew
what to say to me."

"Buck-buck."

"Did you hear that?"

asked Mr. Smith.

"Buck-buck."

"What was it?"

asked Mrs. Smith.

"Buck-buck."

"It's Buck-Buck!" yelled Nancy.

Sure enough,

Buck-Buck had come home.

She was sitting in

a rocking chair.

Her feet were tucked under her.

When the Smiths petted her,

she stood up

and flapped her wings.

Something white gleamed

in the darkness.

Buck-Buck had

laid her first egg!

"That's one smart chicken,"
said Mr. Smith proudly.
"Buck-buck," agreed Buck-Buck.

From that time on

nobody had to tell Buck-Buck

to act more like a chicken.

She made a nest

in the rocking chair.

She laid her egg in it

every night.

In the winter
the Smiths built Buck-Buck
a house of her own.
There were two
rocking chairs inside.
One was for Buck-Buck's nest.

The other was the chair
Nancy Smith sat in
every afternoon
when she came to visit.